The

HISTORY

of A

GREAT HOUSE

ORIGIN

of

JOHN JAMESON WHISKEY

. . .

Containing SOME INTERESTING
OBSERVATIONS THEREON Together with

The CAUSES *of*

Its PRESENT SCARCITY

With DRAWINGS
By HARRY CLARKE

· SINE · METU ·

DUBLIN *printed for* JOHN JAMESON *&* SON Ltd
BOW STREET DISTILLERY DUBLIN
and 7 MARK LANE LONDON E.C.
By MAUNSEL *&* ROBERTS LIMITED
MDCCCCXXIV

THE HISTORY OF
A GREAT HOUSE

THE business of John Jameson & Son, like that of most old firms, has in its origin some degree of adventure, almost of romance. One has to go back a long time, nearly two hundred years, to arrive at its beginnings. At that time the Jameson family were settled in Alloa in Scotland, a steady-going old Scottish family. In 1740 was born John Jameson, the first of the line connected with the John Jameson Whiskey. He held the

office of Sheriff Clerk of Clackmannanshire
from about 1770 till his death in 1823.
Desiring to secure the future of his sons,
he visited Ireland some time before 1780.

In the days of His Gracious Majesty
George III. travel was a hazardous enter-
prise.   Ireland was remote from Alloa.
Many were the dangers and discomforts on

the way, delays of days, often of weeks, before a favourable wind permitted the Sailing
Packets to make a Passage.

John Jameson reaped the reward of his
enterprise by obtaining an interest in the
Distillery at Bow Street, Dublin, and by
1780 had established in it his two sons,
John and William.

By 1800 his son, John Jameson, had
obtained entire control of Bow Street
Distillery, and for three generations a
John Jameson succeeded his father in the

Chairmanship of the Company up to the time of Senator the Right Hon. Andrew Jameson, P.C., D.L., the present Chairman and cousin of the third John Jameson.

Thus for practically a century and a half since the days of the first Distiller, John Jameson, the whiskey of that name has been THE PREMIER IRISH WHISKEY, known as " J.J." wherever Irishmen wandered over the face of the earth.

The warehouses in which John Jameson's whiskey was stored have seen the rise and fall of Governments, changes in manners and customs, peace and war, but have ever been

filled with the one great Whiskey alone. The essential quality and flavour of John Jameson's Whiskey are the same to-day as in the days of Grattan's Parliament, for the plant and materials required were settled then, and in essentials have not been altered since It is impossible to improve on the

best, and generations of connoisseurs have confirmed the verdict that John Jameson's Whiskey is the best.

JOHN JAMESON THREE STAR
is the name by which the whiskey is
known, and the following are some of the
reasons why it is universally recognized as
IRELAND'S PREMIER BRAND.

1.—Its PERFECT MATURITY. Not a drop
of a younger age than seven years is permitted to be bottled under the Distillery
label—much being considerably older. Many
whiskies are advertised as very old—every
drop of " J.J." is, and it can be proved.

II.—It is NOT a heavy " all malt " whiskey, but is made from a mash of Barley, malted and unmalted, mixed with wheat and oats.

III.—Its PURITY, made as it is solely from the finest home-grown cereals obtainable, and chosen each harvest with jealous care.

IV.—Its DISTINCTIVE AROMA and bouquet ; not to be mistaken, and keenly relished by the best judges of whiskey.

V.—Its MELLOW FLAVOUR, due to the carefully selected Sherry and plain oak casks in which it lies in the Firm's famous warehouses, slowly maturing year after year.

VI.—Its WHOLESOMENESS, proved by analysis and by the recommendations of the Medical Faculty when prescribing a stimulant. It increases the enjoyment of food and so promotes digestion and assimilation.

VII.—Its UNIFORMITY OF QUALITY, and · the complete absence of adulteration and artificial flavouring of any kind. It is a genuine Whiskey.

VIII.—Its GENERAL MERITS as a beverage, attested by its long continued popularity, always on the increase.

IX.—FINALLY, it is racy of the soil, and as such known the world over, not only at Home but Abroad, and in all the Dominions.

A COMPLAINT

THERE is but one complaint alleged against John Jameson's Whiskey, and that is really far more of a compliment than a complaint. There is not enough of it.

During the war, distilling was suspended for almost two years and as " John Jameson " cannot be bottled under the Distillery label unless EVERY DROP IS SEVEN YEARS OLD, or older, this has created a shortage of stocks of matured whiskey of the required age. In consequence sales have to be restricted to maintain the quality.

It is regretted that the scarcity will continue for a few years, but in 1926 and 1927 and thereafter it will be possible to meet on a

more liberal scale orders for JOHN
JAMESON & SON'S THREE STAR
WHISKEY.

·SINE· ·METU·

Harry Clarke and "The History of a Great House"

Harry Clarke is widely recognized as Ireland's leading stained glass artist and illustrator – arguably one of the greatest of all time. Born in Dublin on March 17, 1889, Clarke began learning his craft alongside his father (Joshua) and brother (Walter) in the family's stained glass business. Gaining notoriety for his glasswork before his work as a book illustrator, Clarke's windows are widely loved and appreciated for their vibrant colors and finely detailed imagery. Examples are mostly found in chapels and museums throughout Ireland and the rest of Europe. His masterwork, the "Geneva Window", is on display in Miami's Wolfsonian Museum.

Clarke's glasswork consisted largely of pious themes and images but his illustrative work took on decidedly more secular themes. His first published effort were illustrations included in a 1916 edition of "Fairy Tales of Hans Christian Andersen" which was quickly followed by a new edition of Poe's "Tales of Mystery and Imagination". Original and reprinted copies of either book are widely available but two of his next works are not. Dublin whiskey distiller,

John Jameson & Sons, was facing production and supply difficulties for 1924 and 1925 that were rooted in the industry-wide shutdown brought on by World War I in 1917 and 1918. During that period, distilleries across the United Kingdom were nearly entirely shuttered or repurposed as industrial chemical distillers to support the war effort. Some distilleries were used as munitions and supply storage as well. The situation of the Dublin whiskey distillers – Jameson's included – were no different as potable spirit production ground to a halt for the 1917 and 1918 distilling seasons.

Jameson's renowned Three-Star whiskey had long been promised to be a minimum age of 7 years as a commitment to its quality. As 1924 approached (7 years on from 1917), Jameson's realized they would need to reach into their older stock to maintain their pledge meaning higher production costs as well as pulling from a more limited supply than usual. Distribution and profit would suffer. To address this with the consumer and as a clever way to keep the Jameson's brand in front of the public, Harry Clarke was commissioned to illustrate a pamphlet extolling the virtues of Jameson's whiskey and explaining how the war's production interruption were causing their present day shortages. This project became "The History of a Great House" subtitled, "Origins of John Jameson Whiskey Containing Some Interesting Observations Thereon Together With the Cause of its Present Scarcity." The book was produced in February and March of 1924 with printing by Maunsel & Roberts following immediately in April. It was distributed later that year at the Jameson display of the International Advertising Convention held at London's Olympia from July through October, 1924.

The book and Clarke's illustrations were celebrated and appreciated by all who were lucky to receive a copy. Jameson's was pleased with its effectiveness but Clarke was disappointed in the result. He had taken issue with the quality of the printing of this first book which was not up to his standard. Approached for a second Jameson's book in December of 1924, Clarke was initially resistant due to his first experience and workload at the time. The two parties were able to come to an agreement with Jameson's addressing of the printing issues (sourcing Goodridge, Ltd. this time) and Clarke's scheduling of the Jameson's work to alternate with his illustrations for Goethe's "Faust". This second work was entitled "Elixir of Life: Being a Slight Account of the Romantic Rise to Fame of a Great House." This book is even more rare and collectable than "The History of a Great House" and features not only Clarke's illustrations but narrative by Geoffrey Warren (the writing credit for "The History of a Great House" is generally listed as John Jameson & Sons). It was printed in June for distribution at 1925's International Advertising Convention just as "The History of a Great House" was the year before.

1926 and onward would see Jameson's production return to normal and the brand continue on in a healthy manner as it has grown to be one of today's best-known whiskeys of any type, worldwide. Harry Clarke was not as fortunate. Suffering from poor health most of his life, he was diagnosed with tuberculosis in 1929. While traveling back to Ireland from a convalescent resort in Davos, Switzerland, Clarke succumbed to his illness on January 6, 1931, in Chur, Switzerland. He is buried in that same Swiss town.

2017 edition: Aaron Barker Publishing. Carmel, Indiana, USA
All new material including Afterword ©Aaron Barker
ISBN: 978-0-9992024-0-1
whiskywheels@gmail.com

Other works from
Aaron Barker Publishing

The Whisky Distilleries of the United Kingdom
Alfred Barnard

British and Foreign Spirits
Charles Tovey

A Ramble Through Classic Canongate
Alfred Barnard

Condensing and Cooling in Pot-Still and
Patent-Still Distillation
J.A. Nettleton

A Visit to Watson's Dundee Whisky Stores
(with discussion about the 1906 Dundee Whisky Fire, other
whisky fires and the operations of John Robertson & Son)
Alfred Barnard

The History of a Great House
John Jameson & Harry Clarke

Dublin Whisky, Genuine and Spurious
John Jameson, et al.

Dublin Whisky, Report of the Late Trial,
Roe v. The Dublin Whisky Distillery Co.
George Roe & Co.

(coming in 2017 or after)
Joseph Scarisbrick's Revenue Series.
Beer Manual: History and Technical
Spirit Manual: History and Technical
Hydrometry and Spirit Values

www.ingramcontent.com/pod-product-compliance
Lightning Source LLC
Chambersburg PA
CBHW061654050426
42443CB00027B/3298